Collaborating for Chang

M000110648

EDITED BY PEGGY HOLMAN AND TOM DEVANE

Future Search

MARVIN WEISBORD
AND SANDRA JANOFF

BERRETT
BK COMMUNICATIONS
KOEHLER

Berrett-Koehler Communications, Inc.
450 Sansome Street, Suite 1200
San Francisco, CA 94111-3320

ORDERING INFORMATION

Please send orders to Berrett-Koehler Communications, P.O. Box 565, Williston, VT 05495. Or place your order by calling 800-929-2929, faxing 802-864-7626, or visiting www.bkconnection.com.
Special discounts are available on quantity purchases. For details, call 800-929-2929. See the back of this booklet for more information and an order form.

 Printed in the United States of America
on acid-free and recycled paper.

CONTENTS

Voices That Count: Realizing the Potential of Change

. . . .

Peggy Holman and Tom Devane

As seen through the lens of history, change is inevitable. Just look at any history book. Everything from fashions to attitudes has changed dramatically through the years. Change reflects underlying shifts in values and expectations of the times. Gutenberg's invention of the movable type printing press in the fifteenth century, for example, bolstered the developing humanism of the Renaissance. The new technology complemented the emerging emphasis on individual expression that brought new developments in music, art, and literature. Economic and political shifts paralleled the changing tastes in the arts, creating a prosperous and innovative age—a stark contrast to the preceding Middle Ages.

On the surface, technology enables greater freedom and prosperity. Yet this century has overwhelmed us with new technologies: automobiles, airplanes, radios, televisions, telephones, computers, the Internet. What distinguishes change today is the turbulence created by the breathtaking pace required to assimilate its effects.

In terms of social change, one trend is clear: People are demanding a greater voice in running their own lives. Demonstrated by the American Revolution and affirmed more recently in the fall of the Berlin Wall, the riots in Tiananmen Square, the social unrest in Indonesia, and the redistribution of power in South Africa, this dramatic shift in values and expectations creates enormous potential for positive change today.

So, why does change have such a bad reputation?

One reason is that change introduces uncertainty. While change holds the possibility of good things happening, 80 percent of us see only its negative aspects.[1] And even when people acknowledge their current situation is far from perfect, given the choice between the devil they know or the devil they don't, most opt for the former. The remedy we are learning is to involve people in creating a picture of a better future. Most of us are drawn toward the excitement and possibility of change and move past our fear of the unknown.

Another reason we are wary of change is that it can create winners and losers. Clearly the British were not happy campers at the end of the American Revolution. In corporations, similar battle lines are often drawn between those with something to lose and those with something to gain. The real challenge is to view the change *systemically* and ask what's best for both parties in the post-change environment.

Finally, many people have real data that change is bad for them. These change survivors know that "flavor of the month" change initiatives generally fall disappointingly short. In our organizations and communities, many people have experienced the results of botched attempts at transformational change. Like the cat that jumps on a hot stove only once, it's simple human nature to avoid situations that cause pain. And let's face it, enough change efforts have failed to create plenty of cynicism over the past ten years. For these people, something had better "smell" completely different if they're going to allow themselves to care.

Ironically, as demands for greater involvement in our organizations increased, leaders of many well-publicized, large-scale change efforts moved the other way and totally ignored people. They chose instead to focus on more visible and seemingly easier-to-manage components such as information technology, strategic architectures, and business processes. Indeed, "Downsize" was a ubiquitous battle cry of the nineties. According to a 1996 *New York Times* poll, "Nearly three-quarters of all households have had a close encounter with layoffs since 1980. In one-third of all households, a family member has lost a job, and nearly 40 percent more know a relative, friend, or neighbor who was laid off."[2] The individual impact has been apparent in the increased stress, longer working hours, and reduced sense of job security chronicled in virtually every recent book and article on change.

To paraphrase Winston Churchill, "Never before in the field of human endeavors was so much screwed up by so few for so many." By ignoring the need to involve people in something that affects them, many of today's popular change methods have left a bad taste in the mouths of "change targets" (as one popular methodology calls those affected) for *any* type of change. They have also often left behind less effective organizations with fewer people and lower morale. Consequently, even well-intentioned, well-designed change efforts have a hard time getting off the ground.

If an organization or community's leaders *do* recognize that emerging values and rapidly shifting environmental demands call for directly engaging people in change, they often face another challenge. When the fear of uncertainty, the potential for winners and losers, and the history of failures define change, how can they systematically involve people and have some confidence that it will work? That is where this booklet comes in.

A Way Through

This booklet offers an approach that works because it acknowledges the prevailing attitudes toward change. It offers a fresh view based on the possibility of a more desirable future, experience with the whole system, and activities that signal "something different is happening this time." That difference systematically taps the potential of human beings to make themselves, their organizations, and their communities more adaptive and more effective. This approach is based on solid, proven principles for unleashing people's creativity, knowledge, and spirit toward a common purpose.

How can this be? It does so by filling two huge voids that most large-scale change efforts miss. The first improvement is *intelligently involving people* in changing their workplaces and communities. We have learned that creating a collective sense of purpose, sharing information traditionally known only to a few, valuing what people have to contribute, and inviting them to participate in meaningful ways positively affects outcomes. In other words, informed, engaged people can produce dramatic results.

The second improvement is a *systemic* approach to change. By asking "Who's affected? Who has a stake in this?" we begin to recognize that no change happens in isolation. Making the interdependencies explicit enables shifts based on a common view of the whole. We can each play our part while understanding our contribution to the system. We begin to understand that in a change effort the "one-party-wins-and-one-party-loses" perception need not necessarily be the case. When viewed from a systemic perspective, the lines between "winners" and "losers" become meaningless as everyone participates in cocreating the future for the betterment of all. The advantages are enormous: coordinated actions and closer relationships lead to simpler, more effective solutions.

The growing numbers of success stories are beginning to attract attention. Hundreds of examples around the world of dramatic and sustained increases in organization and community performance now exist.[3] With such great potential, why isn't everyone operating this way? The catch with high-involvement, systemic change is that more people have their say. Until traditional managers are ready to say yes to that, no matter how stunning the achievements of others, these approaches will remain out of reach for most and a competitive advantage for a few.

Our Purpose

This booklet describes an approach that has helped others achieve dramatic, sustainable results in their organization or communities. Our purpose is to provide basic information that you can use to decide whether this approach is right for you. We give you an overview including an illustrative story, answers to frequently asked questions and tips for getting started. We've also given you discussion questions for "thinking aloud" with others and a variety of references to learn more.

There is ample evidence that when high involvement and a system-wide approach are used, the potential for unimagined results is within reach. As Goethe so eloquently reminds us, "Whatever you can do or dream you can, begin it. Boldness has genius, power, and magic in it."

What are you waiting for?

RIDING THE ROLLER COASTER

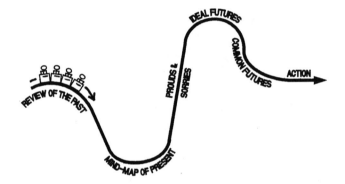

Future Search

Nobody can force change on anyone else. It has to be experienced. Unless we invent ways where paradigm shifts can be experienced by large numbers of people, then change will remain a myth.

—ERIC TRIST

Whole Foods Market CEO John Mackey wanted a shared vision, strategic direction, and set of action plans for his company. The year was 1988. Whole Foods consisted of eight natural foods supermarkets, mostly in Texas; 600 employees; and $45 million in revenues. He organized a future search called "Where We Be in '93" that included team members, team leaders, vendors, suppliers, board members, management, and customers from each store. Participants envisioned a fivefold growth in the business as central to their mission of providing healthy food to people (24 stores and $223 million in sales). They committed to using local organic producers, to setting aside a percentage of profits for environmental causes, and to engaging the community in healthy lifestyle education.

Five years later, having exceeded its growth, revenue, and social goals (32 stores, $240 million in sales, community action budgets in every store), Whole Foods held another future search called "We Be Great in '98." Present were the same stakeholder groups, including people from three newly acquired natural foods chains. The challenge, they said, would be in learning from each other, preserving the local identity of various stores, and building a corporate culture that reflected the best of all members and made the corporate values of customer and community service, knowledgeable team members, and a commitment to healthy food and healthy living cornerstones for the future that were not to be compromised by rapid growth.

In October 1998, 140 people from 87 stores around the United States gathered in Estes Park, Colorado. The company now had 16,000 employees, $1.5 billion in revenues, and regional offices in most parts of the country. Many of its top executives had been there from the start. Once again they addressed the issues of growth, high quality, and their mission, now framed as "Whole Foods, Whole People, and Whole Planet." Their conference—"What We See for 2003"—addressed the many dilemmas of customer service, team development, and succession planning in a giant company growing 25 percent a year. In particular, they focused on how to maintain the core values that had made them successful—including support for organic farming, food safety, and nutritional and health education—while responding to the pressures for growth and globalization of the business.

In a recent CEO's conference, John Mackey was asked how his fast-growing company, which had defined a new niche in the supermarket industry, pulled together strategic planning and gained commitment in such a far-flung, decentralized business. "We hold a future search conference every five years," he said.

People in businesses, communities, and nonprofits all over the world use future search to transform their capability for action. They do it in a few days by involving a "whole system" in the same room working together on a task chosen in advance by a planning committee. Diverse groups explore their past, present, and future; confirm shared values; and commit to action plans. Everybody participates and shares leadership. The most significant changes occur in planning, when people agree to a set of unfamiliar meeting conditions. The key to the success of the method is matching the overall purpose with the right people needed to ensure action.

The Basics

Why future search? As a society we have painted ourselves into a technological corner. We have more ways to do things than ever before. Yet a lot of what matters to us is not getting done, despite the large sums we spend. We experience high walls between haves and have-nots, experts and amateurs, leaders and followers. In future search meetings we take down the walls. We take control of our own futures. We take back responsibility for ourselves. We discover that we can learn from and work with people from many walks of life.

In a future search we become more secure knowing firsthand where other people stand. We discover resources in ourselves and others that we didn't know were there. We begin to accept our differences—in background, viewpoints, and values—as realities to be lived with, not problems to be solved. We are more likely to let go of stereotypes. New relationships emerge. Surprising projects become possible. Future search is a simple way of meeting that has profound implications for organizations and communities everywhere.

Future search brings systems thinking to life. The method provides people a way of acting systemically. By uniting diverse parties who are each other's "environment," we enable people to experience themselves connected to a larger whole rather than talk about it as something "out there." When people all talk about the same elephant, putting together their perceptions of the head, tail, trunk, legs, and tusks, they enable actions that none of them previously thought possible.

Too Good to Be True? Data Suggest an Emphatic No!

Now, it is against common sense that much implementation would flow from one short planning meeting among people who have not met before. Yet this unusual, ongoing action, often on intractable issues, has been documented worldwide following future searches. We believe that this could not be happening unless future search enabled people to use skills they already have—skills always there and rarely accessible in more familiar structures.

We have found that extraordinary results happen when groups assemble and follow just a few key principles, namely,

- have the right people in the room—that is, a cross section of the whole system;
- create conditions where participants experience the whole "elephant" before acting on any part of it;
- seek and build upon common ground;
- take responsibility for learning and action.

Uses of Future Search

Future search has been used to help diverse groups find common ground and develop plans based on that common ground. Some examples are shown in Table 1.

The Process

Our conferences typically involve 60 to 80 people. We consider 64 an optimum number—eight groups of eight. Our purpose is always joint action toward a desired future for X—that is, a community, organization, or issue.

We do five tasks in the approximate time frames shown below.

Day 1 Afternoon	Task 1—Focus on the Past
	Task 2—Focus on the Present, External Trends
Day 2 Morning	Task 2 Continued—Stakeholder Response to External Trends
	Task 2 Continued—Focus on the Present, Owning Our Actions

Day 2 Afternoon	Task 3—Ideal Future Scenarios
	Task 4—Identify Common Ground
Day 3 Morning	Task 4 Continued—Confirm Common Ground
	Task 5—Action Planning

The Focus on the Past, Ideal Future Scenarios, and Confirm Common Ground tasks are done in mixed groups, each a cross section of the whole. The Focus on the Present task is done by "stakeholder" groups whose members have a shared perspective. The Identify Common Ground task is the business of the whole conference. Action Planning employs both existing and voluntary groups. Every task includes a total group dialogue.

The task sequence and group composition are not optional. These set up powerful dynamics that can lead to constructive outcomes. We experience the conference's peaks and valleys as an emotional roller-coaster ride, swooping down into the morass of global trends, soaring to idealistic heights in an ideal future. Uncertainty, anxiety, and confusion are necessary by-products. So are fun, energy, creativity, and achievement. Future search relies on a counterpoint between hope and despair. We believe good contact with our ups and downs leads to realistic choices. In a future search we live with the inevitability of differences, the recognition that no meeting design can reconcile them, and the acknowledgment that people are capable of riding the roller coaster to important new action plans without "more data" or "more dialogue" if they agree to keep working together.

Economic Benefits

In the business world there is no way to calculate the benefits of future search in economic terms. Indeed, these conferences make possible levels of integration not achievable by other means at any cost. In the Hayworth Inc. future search, employees, customers, and suppliers in dialogue with company members discovered and solved a waste-disposal packaging

Groups Searching for Common Ground	Specific Use of the Future Search
Bay State Skills Corporation technical assistance program, small and medium-size manufacturers, public and private service providers, and state government	Participants developed plans to create a centralized extension service to help small and medium-size manufacturers become more competitive. Their plans for coordinated services sparked political action that resulted in a $1 million state grant and a $10 million federal grant.
Inuit people of the Arctic region, land claims organizations, territorial and federal governments, banks, business firms, a mining company, aboriginal funding organizations, and other aboriginal groups	Participants developed an economic-development framework and action plan for education and training, social development, preservation of culture and language, development of small business and industry, investments, organizational development, transportation and infrastructure, renewable resource development, and protection of the environment.
Teachers, students, school administrators, citizens, commissioners, police, firefighters, highway officials, town department heads, and business leaders of Hopkinton, Massachusetts	Participants developed a plan for "Hopkinton 2000 A.D." which addressed thorny issues such as the town's doubling in size between 1977 and 1992, a tax-limiting referendum that left education and other budgets level-funded for three years, and a 6 percent-a-year inflation rate that eliminated contractual raises for school employees. Within a year of the conference, residents raised the school budget 12 percent, and a local business firm partnered with the high school and donated $350,000 worth of computers, technology, and teacher training and pledged $300,000 for the next two years. A 1998 follow-up reports that the town maintains double-digit increases to the school budget and has an ongoing partnership with local businesses which continues to provide approximately $150,000 a year to the system in support of libraries, technology, and teacher training. Henry Fredette, superintendent of the Water Department at the time of the future search, now on the Board of Selectmen, said, "We have succeeded in doing everything we set out to do." The most recent approvals include a $34.7 million high school and a master plan to preserve open space and scenic roads.

The Alliance for Employee Growth and Development (a nonprofit venture of the Communications Workers of America, the International Brotherhood of Electrical Workers, and AT&T)	The Alliance empowers AT&T workers displaced by technology to develop new skills and build their careers. The board—senior executives from the three partners—now conducts board meetings around the country based on future search principles. In these meetings the board convenes local employers and representatives from government, education, and social services in order to help them develop action plans for the mutual benefit of all.
Union officials and senior management from 3M Company's St. Paul Area Plant Engineering organization	Participants helped forward the common purposes of union and management to improve the quality of work life, productivity, and management practice. The groups defined the concept of "Unity Through Partnership" by working together in a future search. They produced a joint vision of a workplace redesigned around customer needs and devised processes for including people who did not attend. Plant Engineering subsequently moved into a large-scale redesign effort, with union and management working together, that included hundreds of employees.
Kansas City, Missouri, community members interested in youth empowerment; services integration, funding, regional collaboration, technology, and volunteer youth programs	Participants implemented the community consensus reached earlier in Kansas City to become "The Child Opportunity Capital." Some key outcomes: Children's Mercy Hospital put young people on boards dealing with oversight and procedures; a local Junior League chose youth empowerment as its next four-year community commitment, offering 90 volunteers and a $200,000 activities grant including an annual future search involving young people.

Table 1. Uses of Future Search

problem that could have taken months in task forces and that may be worth millions of dollars at many levels of the economy. They reduced both cost and environmental impact in a few hours. However, this was only one of dozens of key issues addressed in the future search. When people discover new forms of cooperation, then time, energy, and resources are used profitably.

In addition, these conferences generate dollars that were not previously available. Examples include Bay State Skills; Hopkinton, Massachusetts; and Kansas City, Missouri, cited in the cases above. Many times we have seen money flow from haves to have-nots in an eye blink once people join in making realistic commitments. In one California conference a major foundation executive offered substantial financial support for an action plan that he said would not have been considered if it had come through regular channels. In an eastern city a deputy from the mayor's office offered a community $2 million in public funds, which, she said, had sat idle for lack of any practical plans for its use—until now. These examples are the tip of a very large iceberg that could, if fully understood, turn our assumptions about how to assure wise use of money, public and private, in constructive new directions.

Getting Started

In a future search we seek to take that first important step by

- getting the "whole system" in the room,
- creating a learning environment for participants to experience the whole system,
- searching for common ground from which to build action plans,
- asking individuals to take responsibility to act on the common ground articulated.

The change begins in the planning. Future search requires no training, inputs, data collection, or diagnoses. People face each other rather than concepts, expert advice, or assumptions about what they lack and should do. The method involves comparing notes and listening, sometimes to a mishmash of assumptions, misinformation, stereotypes, and judgments rattling around in all of us. Amazingly, it is not necessary to straighten all this out to succeed. Commitment builds as we encounter chaos together, hang on despite our anxiety, and come out the other side with some good ideas, people we can trust, and faith in our ability to work together. In short, we uncover buried potential that already exists.

Roles and Responsibilities

Table 2 describes the key roles and their responsibilities before, during, and after the future search.

Shifts in Organizational Power and Authority

During the future search conference, participants work as peers as they build the information base, communicate what they learn, make decisions and prepare action plans. After the conference there may or may not be formal changes in power and authority throughout the organization or community. Such changes would depend on the future search action plans and their subsequent implementation.

Conditions for Success

Our conference design embodies a set of mutually reinforcing practices:

- getting the "whole system" in the room,
- all looking at the same "elephant" before working on any part of it (e.g., thinking globally before acting locally),
- exploring current reality and common futures, not problems and conflicts,
- self-managing your own groups and action plans,
- attending the whole meeting,
- meeting under healthy conditions,

	Before	*During*	*After*
Sponsor	• Become clear about the risks and benefits • Decide what you hope to accomplish and how future search applies • Provide support and assurance that you believe in what people are doing	• Be a participant. Share your learnings • Empower people to act	• Have periodic review meetings that bring together stakeholders from the original conference and other interested parties
Designer/ Facilitator	• Help people decide if future search will serve their needs • Help sponsors gather the necessary information, courage, and resources to proceed	• Manage tasks and time • Keep purpose front and center • Encourage self-management and responsibility • Allow the uncertainty until people decide what they will and will not do together • Help people resolve the struggle between old patterns and new paths	• Facilitate a review meeting six months after the conference
Steering Committee	• Frame the conference task • Get the right people in the conference • Set the planning time horizons		
Participants		• Take ownership of your past, present, and future • Confirm mutual values • Search for common ground • Develop independent or joint action plans based on the established common ground • Share leadership	• Take responsibility and follow through with your plans

Table 2. Roles and Responsibilities

- working across three days (i.e., "sleeping twice"),
- taking responsibility publicly for follow-up.

If we want to help people act boldly and creatively, we have to get out of the way. So we do not strive to reduce complexity to a few manageable issues, to resolve disagreements, or to solve long-standing problems. Nor do we give people management models for organizing their varied perceptions. Instead, participants engage in a series of open dialogues on where they've been, where they are, and what they want to do. Future searches often include total strangers or people with a history of conflict who come with confusing and contradictory information. As they experience each other's diverse agendas, they realize that change means accepting each other where they are if they are to go forward together. Those who stay the course find that quick action is inevitable.

What We Can't Do with Future Search

Shore Up Ineffective Leaders

We cannot make up for weak leadership with a future search. A worldwide religious service organization's lawyer wanted to head off a drive to unionize by disgruntled central staff. A reluctant CEO went along with the "legal" advice to sponsor a future search that would enable people to devise the workplace they wanted. People welcomed a chance to make their own plans. They were not surprised, though, when the boss acted on none of them. Nor was their attorney surprised when the staff voted in a union to fill the leadership vacuum.

Convince Skeptics to Go Forward

We have had no success "selling" future search to people paralyzed by worry about losing control. One troubled corporate giant planned to put thousands of people through a training event staged by a prestigious business institute. To the staff's proposal that the company substitute future searches—on the theory that people could get the company out of the box if given a chance—top management turned a deaf ear. Nobody could imagine anything useful happening that wasn't prescribed by experts. They opted for expert training. But nothing new happened. Having two years to "transform the culture or die," they gave up on training their way out of trouble after a year. Several separate departments ran successful future searches, but the company as a whole continued its downward slide.

Reconcile Values Differences

We don't know how to reconcile intractable values differences through future search. When people disagree about deep-seated religious, ethical, or political beliefs that they hold sacred, a future search is unlikely to help them reconcile their beliefs. In a school conference, people brought up highly charged feelings about sex education. The differences between those who did and did not want a particular curriculum were fierce, deeply felt, and long-standing. The parties believed each other to be wrong. At the same time, they agreed on a host of other goals, such as better use of school facilities and more involvement of parents in learning and teaching. They found that they were not going to work out their moral values in this forum but that they had a priceless chance to make progress on matters of benefit to all if they cooperated.

Change Team Dynamics

We can create new dynamics quickly only if we bring together a new group and give it a *new* task. Systems expert Russell Ackoff pointed out long ago that systems change only in relation to the larger systems of which they are a part. That explains why peer-only events—training, T-groups, team meetings—have little effect on the larger system. This seems to be true even when the narrow group does a broad task, such as "scanning the environment." So our guiding principle is always the "whole system" in the room.

Using future search work sheets, for example, a consultant ran a single department through its past, present, and future. To make sure everybody "got it," she included a trust questionnaire and data feedback. "Same old stuff" was the word after the conference from the participants, who neither trusted nor distrusted each other more, although they had learned to trust consultants less. Same people + new inputs = same interactions.

Theoretical Basis

Future search is based on solid, proven theories about how people can best develop plans in groups. While practitioners of future search continue to enhance the conduct of the process, the process is based on just a few simple, but high-leverage principles.

Historical Roots

Our main sources of inspiration come from parallel innovations on both sides of the Atlantic. One is Ronald Lippitt and Eva Schindler-Rainman's large-scale community futures conferences in North America during the 1970s. Another is the pioneering work of Eric Trist, an Englishman, and Fred Emery, an Australian, in developing the Search Conference (hence the name future search). From Lippitt and Schindler-Rainman we learned to get the whole system in the room and focus on the future, not on problems and conflicts. From Trist and Emery we learned the importance of thinking globally before acting locally and of having people manage their own planning. We share with all of them a commitment to democratic ideals and their embodiment of the "action research" tradition of the famed social psychologist Kurt Lewin.

People, Whole Systems, and Planning

We see future search as a learning laboratory for "getting everybody to improve whole systems."[2] It is not the complete answer to anything. Yet the dynamics apply to many kinds of meetings and change strategies.

To experience this method in a single meeting is to open many new doors for future action. We have chosen to stay with lowercase letters to emphasize that future search is not a "thing" carved in stone but a set of principles and opportunities for learning and action. Our society has hardly begun to explore what we can do with diverse parties working on the same task despite their differences.

Future searches enable us to experience and accept polarities. They help us learn how to bridge barriers of culture, class, age, gender, ethnicity, power, status, and hierarchy by working as peers on tasks of mutual concern. The future search process interrupts our tendency to repeat old patterns—fighting, running away, complaining, blaming, or waiting for others to fix problems. And it gives us a chance to express our highest ideals.

Instead of trying to change the world or each other, we change the conditions under which we interact. *That* much we can control, and changing the conditions leads to surprising outcomes.

In future search, major systemic changes occur in the planning process. A diverse group of 6 to 10 people meets from a few days to a few months. They agree on a task and invite a spectrum of stakeholders. They also agree to a novel set of conditions, e.g., meeting for 16 hours over three days, skipping speakers and expert input, putting off action until near the end, and working interactively. In a meeting structured this way, people discover new capabilities no matter what agendas come up. This opens the door to new, unpredictable, highly desired, and long-lived cooperative action that is a high order of systems change.

We don't work to improve relationships among people or functions. Rather, we set up conditions under which people can choose new ways of relating. We don't abstract out social issues (e.g., diversity, trust, communications, collaboration) from economic and technical issues. We are unlikely to run a conference on "the future of diversity in X." Rather, we'd propose that a diverse group of people explore together what kind of X they want to live and work in. Whatever people's skills, education, or experience, they already have what they need to engage in this process. As facilitators, our main job is to maintain boundaries of time and task and to make sure that all points of view are supported.

Sharing the Work

Ours is an encounter with the whole—self, community, organization. But we do not provide an expert systems analysis. Instead, we set up a situation that involves the whole person on many levels. People experience themselves in action as part of a larger whole. They talk over issues they have not raised before with people they have never met. They take responsibility for matters previously avoided or ignored. They dramatize ideal futures as if they have actually happened, thus anchoring them in their bodies. They identify what they *really* want. They voluntarily commit to actions made possible only because of the other people in the room.

Our procedures evolved while working mainly with people who can read and write. However, the underlying principles do not depend on literacy. We believe this work could be done entirely with spoken and/or symbolic communication. The results have been repeated in many cultures and in culturally diverse groups. Indeed, *any* techniques that help people explore their whole system, experience their common stakes, share their ideals, internalize the experience, and take responsibility for what happens are worth applying.

A Learning Laboratory

We believe conferences designed according to the principles we have adopted lead to (1) more participants taking personal responsibility, (2) faster implementation of action plans, and (3) longer-lasting relationships across key boundaries. For now this is a tantalizing hypothesis—

an unproved theory. The only way to test it is to find out what participants do afterward that they couldn't do before. Enough good stories abound to keep us going on this path. So for us, future search is a learning laboratory.

How Future Search Differs from Organizational Development

We see many differences between future search and traditional organization development (OD) meetings. First, OD was conceived not as a single meeting but rather as a strategy for large-scale systemic change. Future search describes a process for one meeting lasting fewer than three days. Second, where OD depended on many people accepting the "need for change," future search depends on 64 people accepting an invitation to spend a few days together.

Third, OD was based on diagnosing gaps between what is and what ought to be. Consultants applied a diagnostic framework, did interviews or surveys, and used the information to create dissonance between what people did and what they said. This was intended to "unfreeze" a system, leading people to reorder their ways of working. Consultants prescribed action steps to close the gaps. Nearly always these involved training, based on the theory that people did not know how to do what they said they wanted to do.

A final difference from OD concerns our neutral assessment of "current reality." What might be seen through an OD lens as deficiencies to be remedied, we consider part of current reality. We don't judge information as good or bad, complete or sketchy, useful or futile, appropriate or redundant. Whatever people do or say—their words, their behavior, their wishes, and their reactions—belongs to them. Whatever happens is an expression of the stakeholders, for better or worse. We are witnessing in action the best that this system is capable of. We don't expect dramatic individual change, only a change in the action potential within the system. For example, people will not suddenly give up authority/dependency needs because they spent a few days as peers.

But they may learn more about their ability to work together with more shared authority.

Sustaining the Results

The single most worrisome aspect of planning is implementation. No process, however comprehensive, guarantees action. Still, we have seen more plans implemented from future searching than any method either of us has used in 30 years. People act quite apart from whether they had a good time, liked the facilitators, collected handouts, resolved their differences, or felt that they had finished. Nor is success a function of how complete an action-planning format is. People find ways to carry out their plans if they have clear goals, the right people are in the room, and they take the whole ride together. Action requires people who understand and believe in their plans and trust each other enough to join in new steps. We think future search fosters understanding, belief, and commitment.

So, while there are no guarantees, what factors contribute to sustainable results? We believe periodic review meetings that bring together stakeholders from the original conference and other interested parties is a simple, congruent way to keep action planning fresh, connected, and relevant for all. What happens after a future search depends largely on what people sign up to do. No sign-up, no action. The fact is, nobody knows how to get other people to do things they don't want to do. Future search theory holds that we get more implementation when we attend to each stage of the process, giving people ample opportunity to engage each other, create an umbrella of shared values, commit to action steps they believe in, and get together regularly to share what they are doing.

Some Final Comments

We see future search as a building block of theory and practice for a house that will never be finished. Practitioners are infusing future search principles into everything they do and enriching this process with many other perspectives. We cannot compare or contrast what we do with other processes because we believe that all large-group processes are independently valuable. Ours are not the only techniques for accomplishing our goals. They are simply the techniques we know best. The roller-coaster ride is inevitable in human affairs. Conceptual schemes and meeting designs come and go. The business of muddling through life's ups and downs together strikes us as a universal process. We believe future searches are good for us and good for society. We hope this work enables thousands of constructive action projects everywhere.

Notes

. . . .

Introduction

[1] Oakley, Ed, and Doug Krug. *Enlightened Leadership*. Denver, Colo.: Stone Tree Publishing, 1991, p. 38.

[2] The *New York Times, The Downsizing of America*. New York: Times Books, 1996.

[3] Holman, Peggy, and Tom Devane, eds. *The Change Handbook: Group Methods for Shaping the Future*. San Francisco: Berrett-Koehler Publishers, 1999. This book contains over twenty such stories of stellar results from high-involvement, systemic change.

Future Search

[1] Adapted from *Future Search: An Action Guide to Finding Common Ground in Organizations and Communities,* by Marvin R. Weisbord and Sandra Janoff, Ph.D. San Francisco: Berrett-Koehler, 1995.

[2] Weisbord, Marvin R. *Productive Workplaces: Organizing and Managing for Dignity, Meaning, and Community*. San Francisco: Jossey-Bass, 1987, pp. 237–252.

Where to Go for More Information

· ·

Since our focus has been to give you an *introduction* to future search, we want you to know where to go for more information. Here are books, Web sites, and other sources that can help you develop a more in-depth understanding. In addition, we have provided recommendations of works that have influenced us.

Organizations

Future Search Alliance
9 Arthurs Round Table
Wynnewood, PA 19096
(610) 896-9989
(610) 658-5988 (fax)
sjanoff@futuresearch.net (e-mail)
www.futuresearch.net (Web site)
- Training
- Videos, books, and reports
- Facilitation services to for-profit future search conferences

Future Search Alliance (cofounded by Sandra Janoff and Marvin Weisbord) is the for-profit, funding arm of the Future Search Network

Future Search Network (formerly SearchNet)
4333 Kelly Drive
Philadelphia, PA 19129

(800) 951-6333 / 215-951-0328
(215) 849-7360 (fax)
fsn@futuresearch.net (e-mail)
www.futuresearch.net (Web site)
- Training
- Videos, books and reports
- Facilitation services to nonprofit and public sector
  future search conferences

Future Search Network (codirectors Sandra Janoff and Marvin Weisbord) is a voluntary, nonprofit association dedicated to a better world through service, colleagueship, and learning. It began in 1993 and now includes many of the world's most experienced practitioners. We offer future searches anywhere in the world for whatever people can afford to pay.

Future Search References

Weisbord, Marvin. *Productive Workplaces.* San Francisco: Jossey-Bass, 1987.

Weisbord, Marvin, and Sandra Janoff. *Future Search: An Action Guide to Finding Common Ground in Organizations and Community.* San Francisco: Berrett-Koehler, 1995.

Weisbord, Marvin, et al. *Discovering Common Ground,* San Francisco: Berrett-Koehler, 1992.

Videos

Discovering Community, a video of the Santa Cruz Community future search on housing, 1996, Blue Sky Productions, (800) 358-0022.

Search for Quality, a video of the Haworth Furniture Manufacturing future search, 1992, Blue Sky Productions, (800) 358-0022.

Influential Sources

Agazarian, Yvonne. *Systems-Centered Therapy for Groups.* New York: Guilford Press, 1997.

Berman, Maurice. *Coming to Our Senses: Body and Spirit in the Hidden History of the West.* New York: Bantum Books, 1990.

Buzan, Tony. *Using Both Sides of Your Brain.* New York: Dutton, 1976.

Emery, Merrelyn. *Searching: For New Directions, in New Ways for New Times.* Canberra: Australian National University, Centre for Continuing Education, 1982.

Fritz, Robert. *The Path of Least Resistance.* New York: Fawcett Columbine, 1989.

Lawrence, Paul R., and Jay W. Lorsch, with research assistance from James S. Garrison. *Organization and Environment, Managing Differentiation and Integration.* Boston: Harvard Business School Press, 1986.

Schindler-Rainman, Eva, and Ron Lippitt. *Building the Collaborative Community: Mobilizing Citizens for Action.* Riverside, Calif.: University of California Extension, 1980.

Sheldrake, Rupert. *The Presence of the Past: Morphic Resonance and the Habits of Nature.* New York: Vintage Books, 1988.

Weir, John and Joyce Weir. *Self-Differentiation.* Video. Blue Sky Productions, 800-358-0022.

Wheatley, Margaret J. *Leadership and the New Science: Learning About Organization from an Orderly Universe.* San Francisco: Berrett-Koehler, 1992.

Questions for Thinking Aloud

. . . .

To gain additional value from this booklet, consider discussing it with others. Here are some questions you might find useful as you explore future search and its application to your situation.

1. What aspects of future search attract you the most? What aspects concern you? What applications do you see for future search?

2. What business reasons or opportunities for a future search exist in your organization or community? What benefits do you think would result from having a future search?

3. Why future search? Why now?

4. Future search brings a diverse group of people into the room to experience the whole "elephant" before acting. Who are likely to be for and against this perspective on planning, and why? What is each person's stake?

5. Who should the sponsor be, and how would you present this idea? Who should be in on the "should we/shouldn't we" dialogue?

6. Who should be on the planning committee? If you're not sure, who should be involved in making the decision?

7. In your situation, who are the stakeholders?

8. What steps must you take to test whether a future search, with the sponsor and stakeholders you are thinking about, is a realistic possibility?

The Authors

· ·

Marvin Weisbord and Sandra Janoff codirect the Future Search Network (formerly SearchNet), an international, voluntary nonprofit consulting network that helps people apply the principles of future search in communities around the world. They also are cofounders of Future Search Alliance, a consulting group that supports community initiatives through private sector efforts. They are coauthors of *Future Search: An Action Guide to Finding Common Ground in Organizations and Communities* (Berrett-Koehler, 1995), and they put on future search training workshops around the world.

Marvin Weisbord has worked as a consultant to business, education, government, and health care in North America and Scandinavia since 1969. He was a founding partner of the consulting firm Block•Petrella•Weisbord, author of *Organizational Diagnosis* (1978) and *Productive Workplaces* (1987), and creator/editor of *Discovering Common Ground* (1992), a landmark for the practice of open-systems planning methods with large groups.

Sandra Janoff, Ph.D., plans, designs, and leads large system change efforts in school systems, corporations, and communities. She has run future searches with business firms, government agencies, communities, schools, hospitals, and nonprofit agencies, on issues of employment, manufacturing, housing, education, health, and many other topics.

Series Editors

Peggy Holman is a writer and consultant who helps organizations achieve cultural transformation. High involvement and a whole-systems perspective characterize her work. Her clients include AT&T Wireless Services, Weyerhaeuser Company, St. Joseph's Medical Center, and the U.S. Department of Labor. Peggy can be reached at (425) 746-6274 or pholman@msn.com.

Tom Devane is an internationally known consultant and speaker specializing in transformation. He helps companies plan and implement transformations that utilize highly participative methods to achieve sustainable change. His clients include Microsoft, Hewlett-Packard, AT&T, Johnson & Johnson, and the Republic of South Africa. Tom can be reached at (303) 898-6172 or tdevane@iex.net.

The Change Handbook
Group Methods for Shaping the Future
Edited by Peggy Holman and Tom Devane

The Change Handbook presents eighteen proven, highly successful change methods that enable organizations and communities of all shapes and sizes to engage and focus the energy and commitment of all their members These diverse participative change approaches, described in detail by their creators and expert practitioners, illustrate how organizations and communities today can achieve and sustain extraordinary results and foster a capacity to handle the inevitable turbulence along the way. By first systematically involving all organizational stakeholders in the change process, and then planning and implementing change simultaneously—in real time—these methods uniquely enable all members to become change agents, active participants in determining their organization's direction and future.

Marvin Weisbord, Merrelyn Emery, Masaaki Imai, Kathie Dannemiller, Harrison Owen, and many other leading thinkers and practitioners of organizational change show how to harness the vision, energy, and enthusiasm of the entire organization—from employees at all levels to key stakeholders to entire communities. In The Change Handbook they provide practical answers to frequently asked questions to that you can choose the methods that will work best in your participative change efforts.

> "In a world where change is the norm, where the effectiveness of organizations is a competitive advantage, and where we have more change methodologies available than most people could absorb in a lifetime, this book has identified how to match the best approach to the situation. While providing structured guidelines for organizational improvement, the authors acknowledge and celebrate the power of creativity and engaged people to provide the energy needed for successful change."
>
> —SUSAN MERSEREAU, Vice President,
> Organizational Effectiveness, Weyerhaeuser Company

Paperback original, approx. 450 pages, ISBN 1-57675-058-2
Item no. 50582-605   U.S. $49.95
To order call 800-929-2929 or visit www.bkconnection.com

Collaborating for Change

Peggy Holman and Tom Devane, Editors

The Collaborating for Change booklet series offers concise, comprehensive overviews of 14 leading change strategies in a convenient, inexpensive format. Adapted from chapters in *The Change Handbook*, each booklet is written by the originator of the change strategy or an expert practitioner, and includes

- An example of the strategy in action
- Tips for getting started
- An outline of roles, responsibilities, and relationships
- Conditions for success
- Keys to sustaining results
- Thought-provoking questions for discussion

If you're deciding on a change strategy for your organization and you need a short, focused treatment of several alternatives to distribute to your colleagues, or you've decided on a change strategy and want to disseminate information about it to get everyone on board, the Collaborating for Change booklets are the ideal choice.

◆ SEARCH CONFERENCE
Merrelyn Emery and Tom Devane
Uses open systems principles in strategic planning, thereby creating a well-articulated, achievable future with identifiable goals, a timetable, and action plans for realizing that future.

◆ FUTURE SEARCH
Marvin R. Weisbord and Sandra Janoff
Helps members of an organization or community discover common ground and create self-managed plans to move toward their desired future.

◆ THE CONFERENCE MODEL
Emily M. Axelrod and Richard H. Axelrod
Engages the critical mass needed for success in redesigning organizations and processes, co-creating a vision of the future, improving customer and supplier relationships, or achieving strategic alignment.

◆ THE WHOLE SYSTEMS APPROACH
Cindy Adams and W. A. (Bill) Adams
Creates a world of work where people and organizations thrive and produce outrageous individual and organizational results.

◆ PREFERRED FUTURING
Lawrence L. Lippitt
Mobilizes everyone involved in a human system to envision the future they want and then develop strategies to get there.

- **THE STRATEGIC FORUM**
Chris Soderquist
Answers "Can our strategy achieve our objectives?" by building shared understanding (a mental map) of how the organization or community really works.

- **PARTICIPATIVE DESIGN WORKSHOP**
Merrelyn Emery and Tom Devane
Enables an organization to function in an interrelated structure of self-managing work groups.

- **GEMBA KAIZEN**
Masaaki Imai and Brian Heymans
Builds a culture able to initiate and sustain change by providing skills to improve process, enabling employees to make daily improvements, installing JIT systems and lean process methods in administrative systems, and improving equipment reliability and product quality.

- **THE ORGANIZATION WORKSHOP**
Barry Oshry and Tom Devane
Develops the knowledge and skills of "system sight" that enable us to create partnerships up, down, and across organizational lines.

- **WHOLE-SCALE CHANGE**
Kathleen D. Dannemiller, Sylvia L. James, and Paul D. Tolchinsky
Helps organizations remain successful through fast, deep, and sustainable total system change by bringing members together as one-brain (all seeing the same things) and one-heart (all committed to achieving the same preferred future).

- **OPEN SPACE TECHNOLOGY**
Harrison Owen (with Anne Stadler)
Enables high levels of group interaction and productivity to provide a basis for enhanced organizational function over time.

- **APPRECIATIVE INQUIRY**
David L. Cooperrider and Diana Whitney
Supports full-voiced appreciative participation in order to tap an organization's positive change core and inspire collaborative action that serves the whole system.

- **THINK LIKE A GENIUS PROCESS**
Todd Siler
Helps individuals and organizations go beyond narrow, compartmentalized thinking; improve communication, teamwork, and collaboration; and achieve breakthrough thinking.

- **REAL TIME STRATEGIC CHANGE**
Robert W. Jacobs and Frank McKeown
Uses large, interactive group meetings to rapidly create an organization's preferred future and then sustain it over time.

Collaborating for Change Order Form

Each booklet comes shrinkwrapped in packets of 6

Order in Quantity and Save!

1–4 packets: $45 per packet • 5–9 packets: $40.50 per packet
10–49 packets: $38.25 per packet • 50–99 packets: $36 per packet

# of Packets		Item #	Price
_____	*Search Conference*	6058X-605	_____
_____	*Future Search*	60598-605	_____
_____	*The Strategic Forum*	60601-605	_____
_____	*Participative Design Workshop*	6061X-605	_____
_____	*Gemba Kaizen*	60628-605	_____
_____	*The Whole Systems Approach*	60636-605	_____
_____	*Preferred Futuring*	60644-605	_____
_____	*The Organization Workshop*	60652-605	_____
_____	*Whole-Scale Change*	60660-605	_____
_____	*Open Space Technology*	60679-605	_____
_____	*Appreciative Inquiry*	60687-605	_____
_____	*The Conference Model*	60695-605	_____
_____	*Think Like a Genius Process*	60709-605	_____
_____	*Real Time Strategic Change*	60717-605	_____

Shipping and Handling _____

($4.50 for the first packet; $1.50 for each additional packet.)

TOTAL (CA residents add sales tax) $_____

Method of Payment

Orders payable in U.S. dollars. Orders outside U.S. and Canada must be prepaid.

❏ Payment enclosed   ❏ Visa   ❏ MasterCard   ❏ American Express

Card no. _____   Expiration date _____

Signature _____

Name _____   Title _____

Organization _____

Address _____

City/State/Zip _____

Phone (in case we have questions about your order) _____

May we notify you about new Berrett-Koehler products and special offers via e-mail?

E-mail _____

Send Orders to Berrett-Koehler Communications, Inc., P.O. Box 565,
Williston, VT 05495 • **Fax** (802) 864-7626 • **Phone** (800) 929-2929
• **Web** www.bkconnection.com